THE MIDDLE EAST TODAY

INTRODUCTION

Edward Ledwich Mitford FRGS (1811-1912) was the doyen of the British Foreign Office - actively engaged in British foreign policy and a colleague of Lord Palmerston. Lord Palmerston (1784-1865) served as both Foreign Secretary and two terms as British Prime Minister. From Edward's student days in Paris and his remarkable aptitude for languages he became fluent in French, Italian and Arabic, and from the age of 18 years, served as British Consul in Morocco and later as Consul in Colombo, Sri Lanka until his retirement in 1866, at the age of 55 years.

After 5 years in Morocco, Edward was offered employment in Colombo, Ceylon, now known as Sri Lanka. Only problem was, how to get there… as he hated travelling by ship? Before telephones existed and photography was invented, aged 28 years, he undertook the most adventurous and perilous journey of his life – to travel overland from London to Colombo, a journey of 10,000 miles overland with 7000 miles on horseback. During his preparation he was approached by a young man of 22 years, Austen Henry Layard, apparently bored with his job in a London legal office, who asked to accompany Edward overland to Colombo. Had this not happened, Layard would most likely have lived a life of dull respectability and would never have risen to become Sir Austen, Under-Secretary of State for Foreign Affairs in the British government, during the reign of Queen Victoria. Layard travelled with Edward as far as Hamadan in Persia, now Iran where they regretfully parted company. Edward continued alone and Layard fell in love with archaeology and the Arab way of life.

The reasons which induced Edward to undertake this amazing journey are best explained by Edward himself.

"In the year 1839, after five year's residence as British Consul and travelling Morocco, I found myself in the unenviable position of being without occupation, when my attention was directed to the probability of employment in the colony of Ceylon, either in the government service or in the newly opened enterprise of farming. To reach Ceylon I must either take the long sea voyage round the Cape or the shorter and inconvenient one via the Mediterranean and the Red Sea, with a caravan across the Isthmus of Suez. But moved by the love of travel, after consulting the map, I resolved to take the journey entirely by land. By taking a south-east line through southern Europe, Central Asia and India, I could reach my destination with no more sea than the Straits of Dover, the ferry across the Bosporus and the Strait of Adam's Bridge, through most interesting and little known country.

SYRIA AS IT WAS

FROM NOTES & LETTERS HOME

The first of a series of five books

THE MIDDLE EAST AS IT WAS

Syria, Palestine, Iraq, Iran and Afghanistan.

Cover page photograph of dove painted by Edward Ledwich Mitford FRGS in 1898.
The original painting is on the ceiling of Mitford Church Bell Tower,
Mitford, Northumberland.

MITFORD LITERARY SOCIETY

SYRIA AS IT WAS

Original title – From England to Ceylon, 7000 miles on horseback, by Edward L Mitford. Published by W H Allen & Co, 13 Waterloo Place, London.1884.

This edition published in 2017 by the Mitford Literary Society
Email address - mitford@orange.fr

A CIP catalogue record for this book is available from the British Library.

ISBN – 978-0-9955839-0-0

Cover page photograph of dove painted by Edward Ledwich Mitford FRGS in 1898. The original painting is on the ceiling of the Mitford Church Bell Tower, Mitford, Northumberland, England.
Edward was elected Fellow of the Royal Geographic Society on 23rd April 1883.

Also on Facebook – Mitford Literary Society & Mitford Dynasty

This is the first of a series of five books on Syria, Palestine, Iraq, Iran and Afghanistan.

Obviously, it was impossible to foresee how long this journey would take and it was clear to me that it must be carried out in the most economical manner. My previous experience among the Arab people taught me that nothing but the appearance of poverty could carry us with any safety through countries where any show of wealth, by exciting the cupidity of the locals, would expose us, if not to the danger of life – to the certainty of being robbed.

When travelling it is necessary to be armed - as an unarmed man is the most helpless animal in creation, and meets with very little respect among lawless and uncivilized people. In preparation, I visited the arms factory at Chaudesfontaines, close to Brussels. The Belgian guns are provided with slings and are very light, and with this slung across my back over endless hours across the many Middle Eastern countries, it was an important consideration. I also carried two small pocket guns, easily hidden and readily accessible".

The reader may like to reflect on the enormity of Edward's undertaking especially when compared to the current circumstances in the Middle East in the 21st century. How many hardships he endured on that long and often tedious journey through practically unknown countries – how, at the risk of health and even life, he had to sleep in sodden clothes under the star-lit sky – how he was delayed by sickness and hunger, and weather bound by rain – how he had to encounter the suspicions of local governments and the cutthroat irresponsibility of thieves and robbers. All this Edward graphically relates so the reader can easily imagine his real life journey.

Edward observed closely, took careful notes from day to day of the countries and people he saw. He got to know all the un-mapped, hidden routes and passages through all the Middle East countries he travelled. Another talent was drawing and painting and some of his sketches are included in some books, like the picture of the dove on the cover of this book. His writing is impressive as you will read.

Questions often received at the time included, how many horses did he use, what money did he carry and what languages were spoken? Apart from walking and the rugged, bone jolting spring-less horse carts, he was able to use hired horses in-between intervals of buying a total of six horses to complete the entire journey. For money, there was a bank at Istanbul and after that he cashed credit-notes with various consular officials along the way. The small eastern coins of gold and silver were convenient to carry and concealment and traveling with one horse with no baggage, his wants and needs were few.

Edward writes with characteristic modesty. Throughout the journey Edward wore English clothes, never attempting any disguise, which would have been both impolite and useless. "Impolite because the open profession of an Englishman, accompanied by ordinary prudence will always be found the greatest safeguard in all eastern countries – useless because in no case have I ever known an Oriental deceived by it".

His knowledge of Arabic was invaluable to him up to a certain point. But it was the Arabic of Morocco that he knew and could speak fluently. Although he found it different from the dialects spoken in Syria and Mesopotamia, (from the ancient Greek, the land between the Tigris–Euphrates river system, corresponding to modern-day Iraq, Kuwait, the north eastern section of Syria and to a much lesser extent south eastern Turkey and smaller parts of south western Iran), the roots of the language being the same, he found it most useful for ordinary purposes. Edward's journey takes us through Syria, Palestine, Iraq, Iran and Afghanistan and took a total of two years and ten months. Arriving in Colombo, the British Governor, Sir Colin Campbell, said "Edward, you are still alive?" This book, the first of five, covers his journey through Syria, in Edward's own words.

At the grand old age of 84 years Edward, and according to the Mitford Estate & Trust Act (of 900 years) by Royal Assent dated 1854, Houses of Parliament, Westminster, London, succeeded to the Mitford estates in Northumberland and Yorkshire, a total of 50,000 acres, without a penny in the bank except his annual, civil service pension. His brother's wife ran off with £46,000 (around £5 million today). He became the 27th Squire of Mitford along the direct line of succession extending back to 1066 and 1042, to manage the Mitford estate of 35,000 acres (approximately 130 square kilometres), with over 26 tenanted farms and around 600 village residents, in addition to the Yorkshire estate of Hunmanby & Filey Bay, for 17 years until his death in 1912. Newcastle International Airport is built on part of the old Mitford estate.

He also served on the Bench of the Morpeth and Newcastle Magistrates court. He wrote and published five books and his gravestone in Mitford churchyard reads, "There the tears of earth are dried - there the hidden things are clear".

PREAMBLE

As opposed to two, large and cumbersome volumes of text written over 100 years ago, by my great-great grandfather Edward Ledwich Mitford, that mostly academics and historians would read, I thought it best to edit and rewrite a series of small, easy to read books that focus on the individual countries covering Edward's amazing journey, taken from notes and letters home to his mother during his nearly three year, horseback journey from London to Colombo, Sri Lanka.

Having spent over 15 years working with horses of all different shapes and sizes in many countries including the Middle East, I'm totally amazed with what he did. His spirit of adventure, resolve and character shines through. Nowadays, things have changed but still work when one has the motivation, guts and ability to make things happen. Apart from horses, a family friend recently chose to ride a bicycle from London to Cape Town. This took 10 months of mind over matter, often across flat and endless desert wilderness with only the sun and sand as a companion. However, with modern technology and endless goodwill along the way it was another remarkable journey of human resolve and spirit (see www.wildbikeride.com).

Back to the future? History helps us to understand our existence and the way forward? Each of these, easy to read books, provides a concise, informative and easily read account of Edward's journey and his genuine opinion of his experiences – the people, culture, facts, politics and actualities of the Arab nations, prior to the breakup of the Ottoman Empire.

Looking through the history of the Middle East from the 1800's, you'll be amazed to discover that many of the names of places and countries are not used anymore and many of these countries have known many different shapes, borders and cultures. It was fascinating to research Edwards's journey especially looking to recent years and conflicts of world powers. It continues like a chess game with a devastating domino effect on western countries and European culture. The Middle East countries were once a fascinating tourist venue, now sadly off limits?

As you may gather, this is more than a simple expedition through what some call the nightmare of the Middle East. This series of five books helps us understand the game play of nations from the First World War. There is more to drawing a simple line in the sand, forgetting the ancient cultures and historical evolution and balance of tribal people and their use of ancient roads, economic exchanges, religion, cultures and languages. The reason the author has republished the work of his great-great grandfather is purely historical and far from any debate. It presents a historical perspective of what the Middle East was like during this period to what it is now.

MITFORD LITERARY SOCIETY

SYRIA AS IT WAS

Edward's journey on horseback through Syria,
took him through the following villages, towns & places.

Tersoos, Cydnus Falls, Aleian Plain, Taurus Mountains, Adana, Messis on the Pyramus River, Kutolak, Bay of Scanderoon, Bayas, Mount Amanus, Alexandretta or Scanderoon, Bylan, Antakia, Suadea, Seleucia Piera, Beityas, Daphne, Kerim, Dana, Tukaat, Aleppo, Palmyra, Kinesrin, Khan Tuman, Sermein, Khaneh Sibl, Marrah, Khan Shokune, Kiffoorbashi, Jebel Anzirie mountains, Taiba, Hamah, Rostan, Tellé, Homs or Hemessa, Eskeli Lake, Heddedee, Kalat el Hosn (fortress), Ain el Haramia, Telebas, Callimone, Shik a Shika, Kalat el M'selha (castle), Batrone, Djouni, Nahr el Kelb, Beirut, Sidon, Saida, Tsoor & Tyre.

It's not easy to define the northern limits of Syria, but it's usually counted to extend to the pass of the Taurus Mountains, called the Sicilian gates, and thus far – it is held by the army of Mohammed Ali under Ibrahim Pasha, whose advanced guard is between Tersoos and Adana. The difference in passing from one jurisdiction to the other is not apparent, and travellers are unmolested and treated with equal consideration.

13 November 1839

After visiting the falls of the Cydnus, we slept at the house of Mr William Barker, who accompanied us the next morning, part of the way to Adana, goshawk on fist, to show us some falconry. We crossed the Aleian plain, the Taurus Mountains rising on our left, the higher parts crowned with snow. The Francolin (Perdix francolinus), a handsome game bird, the upper part of the plumage being spotted with round white spots on a black back ground, is abundant here, and is found in all the intermediate warm districts between here and India, where it is known by the name of the black partridge. The goshawk is a short winged hawk of heavy flight and it never takes his quarry at the first attempt. It alights on the bush where the partridge has sheltered, from which neither will move until the game is once more sprung. Either from the hawk being more excited, or the partridge weaker from fear, it is taken at the second flight.

Adana is a good sized town, and has a pretty appearance from the East, with the river Syhoon or Sarus flowing alongside, through scattered palms, and backed by the bold sweeps of the Taurus Mountains, covered with snow. In the open plain was the camp of Ibrahim Pasha's army, which is strong in artillery, keeping watch on the Turkish frontier. The Egyptian soldiers have a much neater appearance than the Turkish; instead of the slovenly European dress, their uniform is only a modification of the eastern costume of full trousers to the knee, continued with light leggings to the foot, with a dark cloth or linen jacket and red cap. They are armed with a sword, musket and bayonet. They are better made men then the Turks; but, owing to the great mortality from bad and scanty food and exposure, the ranks have been filled up by a large proportion of mere boys, who are torn from their homes and families to gratify the Pasha's love of playing at soldiers, many being brought from the warm plains of Egypt, to brave the bitter cold of the Syrian winters. At Antioch, where the troops amounted to upwards of 7000, the mortality among them was eight per day on an average at this time: more than 40%. It was the sickly season, so I do not suppose that it is always in the same proportion; but the medical practitioners in the Pasha's service assured us that a large majority died of nostalgia or homesickness. In Syria the villages are swept of their inhabitants to supply recruits for the army; and only woman and a few old men are left, who are compelled to cultivate sufficient grain round their ruined villages to supply the wants of the troops. It was even expected that the Christian population would have been included in the conscription.

We lodged with Signor Nani and party, Italian instructors, attached to the troops. They are well paid, but always from 12 to 20 months in arrear, to prevent their leaving the service at their option - so they are compelled to run in debt. We had ridden for nine hours to Adana, and the next day we made seven hours to Messis, a village built on the ruins of a larger place on the top of a mound, on the right bank of the Pyramus River. The sheik of this place was rather unaccommodating, and we had some difficulty in procuring shelter, and were at length obliged to be satisfied with a small stable, which we shared with our horses, at the risk of being trampled on during the night. The plain we passed was flat, with a few palms scattered over it, and abounding in gazelles, that were grazing in herds on either side of our path.

In the morning we crossed the Pyramus river over a long bridge, and passing a range of low mountains, we reached Kurtolak after a six hour ride. Here were the remains of a substantial khan and an old mosque, with a few huts occupied by soldiers. We remained here till midnight, and then continued our ride around the head of the bay of Scanderoon, and at an early hour the next morning we crossed the Pinarus river, which still flows quietly through the field where the fate of Asia was decided.

It is difficult to conceive a more inconvenient situation for marshalling the vast hosts of Darius and Alexander than the battle plain of Issus, were the mountains run down towards the coast, leaving an irregular strip between them and the sea. This strip gradually narrows, until there is only a precipitous path before coming to Bayas, winding over the hills along the coast and the road passes under a tall stone arch of some antiquity. They are also some ruined walls on the cliffs, on the right of the road.

At Bayas there is an old Saracen castle, with its mosque and khan, and an arched stone bazaar, which is very broad but nearly deserted, and we had difficulty in procuring barley for our horses. This place was some time back the stronghold of an independent freebooter, called Kutchuk Ali, whose deeds are still remembered. He commanded all the tribes in the neighbouring mountains, and took payments from travellers. When the Dutch traded goods to Aleppo, their consul, who was on his way to Aleppo, was seized by this bandit and kept prisonor for a long period to extort ransom. The spot is well chosen for the haunt of a robber chief, commanding the Syrian gates. If in need of retreat, he could flee into the mountains.

16 November 1839

Leaving Bayas at midday, we passed a bridge over a mountain stream close to the gates, and crossed a small plain covered with large myrtle bushes, the picturesque verdant slopes of Mount Amanus rising on the left. Nearer to Alexandretta extensive morasses spread out to the foot of the mountains, to which lines of wild geese and ducks were winging their evening flight. The town had a pretty appearance across the calm bay, glowing in a red sunset, with two or three tall palms towering above it in the declining light. We alighted at the house of the Austrian consul, Signor Jonas, the British consul being absent.

The present Alexandretta, or Scanderoon, is now merely a village. It was formerly the port of Aleppo, when the commerce of this part of the Middle East was in the hands of the company of Aleppo merchants: the high walls of their ruined factory now the principal building in the village. The climate exceeds in insalubrity to that of Tersoos, from the same cause, viz, the marshy nature of the surrounding countryside. Its deadly nature has always been notorious, even when a place of more importance, for on reference to the old registers of correspondence of the merchants of Aleppo, who appointed their own consuls, it appears that an application was made nearly every three months for the appointment of a new consul, in consequence of the former having fallen victim to the marsh fever. Alexandretta is now of so little consequence that it is scarcely necessary to maintain a consulate in such an unhealthy locality, while places of more importance, as Tripoli, Acre, Jaffa and others, have merely native agents, entrusted with our national interests.

17 November 1839

After a day of rain we left early the next morning on the 18th, ascending the steep pass of Beilan, over Mount Amanus, the wind blowing half a gale. This wind must have been quite local, either following the north western side of Mount Arsus from the south west, or descending the mountains vertically from the upper strata of the atmosphere; for as soon as we had turned the ridge of the mountain to the opposite descent, it was quiet and suddenly pleasantly calm.

At the summit of this pass, we came on the large village of Bylan, romantically situated in a basin surrounded by peaks and crags, from which streams of water were rushing down through the streets. There are numerous aqueducts carried across the ravines on arches to conduct the water to the different mills and baths, while the waste water precipitates itself from ledge to ledge, finding its way down the ravine which intersects the place. From the height of the Alma Dagh you look down on the plains of Syria, a broad marshy lake lying to the east and the Orontes River winding alongside the town of Antioch, backed by the Anzeiry Mountains. We descended the mountain by a rapid downward slope, and crossing the plain, entered Antakia at dusk by a bridge over the river. The minarets of the mosques rose above the trees, glittering with lamps in honour of a Mohammedan festival, and the plaintive moaning of the large waterwheels, which supply the town with water from the river, added by their melancholy sound to the novelty of the celebrations I experienced on approaching this acclaimed locality.

We found hospitable reception at the house of our native consular agent, Giorgio Adeeb. The modern Antakia is a large Turkish town, with long streets of shops. The houses are mean, and the town extremely dirty, from the accumulation of mud. As a result intermittent fever is very prevalent, and the people are wishing for rain to cleanse the town from filth and sickness at the same time. The place is crowded with soldiers, who, as before mentioned, suffer much due to the unhealthy season.

Ibrahim Pasha has built a handsome large barrack here, the materials for which were taken from the fine old walls of Antioch, a most splendid remnant of antiquity, which this Egyptian destroyer has partly pulled down for the purpose. The masonry, however, was so compact that he was compelled to blast the wall with gunpowder, and then the workmen being unable to detach the stone from the cement, the masses were hewn into blocks as they were, and used in building. These walls run up and crown the heights behind the town, crossing ravines, and, descending the other side, enclosing double the area occupied by the modern town. The eastern entrance is through the massive ancient gateway.

The banks of the Orontes River are lined with extensive gardens and orchards of fruit trees, irrigated from the river, and affording a fine cover for woodcock, which arrive here in great numbers around the beginning of December. The Persian wheels used on the riverbanks to supply the baths and houses are very high, and made to work with the force of the current. With pedals being attached to the outer circumference on which the stream flows, its power is increased by the base of the wall built in the river, and on which the axle rests, forming a canal for the concentration of its force. The wheel itself is made with several hollow wooden boxes or scoops. These fill on their immersion, and empty themselves turning over at the top into a trough, from whence the water is conveyed by canals or pipes to its destination. In the gardens the wheels are turned by oxen, the water being raised from canals cut from the river.

Everything here is sold by weight: wood, oils, grain, and even in a shop, if you have occasion for an ivory comb, it is weighed and delivered to you at so much per ounce.

Having been kindly furnished with letters of introduction from Mr W Barker, of Tersoos, we made a detour to his father's residence at the mouth of the Orontees river, near Suadea. We rode down the valley, which is very fertile and full of Mulberry plantations, and arrived in the evening at Mr Barker's villa, where we experienced a most friendly and cordial welcome from himself and his amiable family.

Mr Barker, who was formally Consul General in Egypt, has resided for upwards of 20 years, since his retirement, on his estates in this beautiful valley, where he has occupied his time with scientific and horticultural pursuits, and surrounded himself with a paradise of fruits and flowers of all countries, which equally thrive in this fine climate. The orange and the citron grow beside the China medlar, or loquat, peaches, and the fruits of northern climes and all arrive at the same perfection.

The situation of this spot is very picturesque, being near the ruins of the old port of Seleucia Piera (from whence St Paul sailed on his first mission to the Gentiles), and backed by a spur of Amanus; whilst in front rises the high conical peak of Mount Cassius, reflected in the blue waters of the bay. This peak is called by the Arabs Jibel Akraa," the bald mountain". There are a few remains of the ancient city, except some fragments of Hellenic masonry, and the Porte, which is now far above the sea level, and partly occupied by a marsh, with some massive ruins of jetties or piers which run out into the sea. This is an additional evidence of the fact remarked at Pompeopolis that the sea has receded from this coast. North of the ruins is an extraordinary Roman work, consisting of a canal sunk in the rock to the depth of 30 feet, and extending a quarter of a mile, for the purpose of conducting a mountain torrent into the sea, which would otherwise have filled the port with debris and alluvium. At the upper end of this canal is a massive wall of large stones, which conducted the water into the tunnel as it descended from the heights.

In a northerly direction lie the catacombs of the city, consisting of a number of tombs excavated in some high cliffs, some of which have defaced inscriptions. There is one large arched columbarium over a central tomb with troughs at the sides for others.

22 November 1839

We made an excursion with our host to one of his estates; about five hours ride in the mountains, where he had a summer villa. The village is called Beityass, and is inhabited entirely by Armenian Christians. From this beautiful spot you look down on the plain of Antioch, while precipitous naked crags rise up in the foreground, and overhead the grapes hang from the trellises in tempting luxuriance, bedewed by the mist of a fountain which casts its sparkling flakes into the sunshine. The lower valleys and sides of the mountains are clothed with myrtle trees covered with snowy blossoms. The ravines are frequented by panthers as formally, "Look from the top of Amana, from the top of Shenir and Hermon, from the lion's dens, from the mountains of the leopards." The lions now found in the valley of the Tigris must have formally been common here, but so many panthers were taken from Cilicia to supply the Roman games that Cicero complains of their rarity in his time.

About ten minutes walk from the house is a wild romantic glen, overshadowed by thick spreading trees, down which flow numerous streams gushing through and over the rocks hung with water plants and creepers. This spot was supposed by a late author to be the site of Daphne, not without some reason, as it answers to the descriptions of history much more nearly than the spot assigned to it on the opposite mountain, on the left bank of the Orontes river. We are informed that the Temple of Apollo at Daphne was surrounded in groves of cyprus and laurel trees (this may probably mean the bay tree, as the laurel is not found in this country) to the exclusion of the sun's rays. The present situation given to Daphne is remarkable for being entirely bare of trees on the open side of the mountain, and has no ruins standing to fix its locality. The temple was burnt in the time of Julian, about 362 A.D. There is an interesting ruin here which gives some probability to the above hypothesis. This is apparently the remains of a church of the era of the Christian emperors: but on examination it is evident that this has been built of the materials of a former and more ancient temple, parts of which, consisting of walls and broken arches, of an entirely different and superior style of architecture, still survive the fall of the two successive superstructures. The ground around is also strewn with mixed ruins. Close to the base of this building is a copious spring of the purest water, issuing from a deep artificial tunnel sunk in the rock, and strongly arched over.

 The principal cultivation of these districts is silk, the greater part of the lands being laid out in mulberry plantations. Mr Barker has imported supplies of the silk-worms eggs' from Piedmont, as the indigenous breed is found to deteriorate and become of little value. The inhabitants, with a few exceptions, are Armenians, and a hardy race of villagers. Mr Barker instanced a case of a woman going down to the river with her washing, and all being done, she brought home her baby on her back and the clothes on her head.

We visited the ruins of a church about twelve miles off, on the opposite mountain, which has been dedicated to Simon Stylites (a Syrian saint who lived for 37 years on top of a pillar). In the centre of the ruins stand the remains of the pillar, on the top of which this man imagined he could atone for his own sins. The pedestal and a portion of the pillar is undetached from the rock of which it forms part. The first is nine feet square and the pillar six feet in diameter, so I have no doubt, if he did not exceed the common stature; he had plenty of room to sleep at his ease. The ruins of the church consist of massive blocks of hewn stone, and would appear to have been overthrown by one of the earthquakes which are so common in this country. We were extremely fortunate in having fine weather during our stay in this lovely valley. On account of the near approach of the rainy season, sufficient vapours were accumulated to produce the most glorious sunsets, which heightened the beauty of the scenery, tinting the broad expanse and the mountain peaks with gold, purple and crimson.

At this late season the trees were clothed with verdure and the fragrant myrtles in full bloom, and growing in the wildest exuberance. Wandering amidst these scenes seemed like the realisation of a poet's dream, and this, with delightful society, openhearted kindness, and intellectual enjoyment, combined to form one of the brightest spots on the dark stream of my wandering existence, and to which I shall ever look back with renewed pleasure.

Here Edward includes a few lines of poetry in remembrance of his time spent there.

"I may not see thee more: yet after times
Will rise upon my weary path thy scenes
Of trancing loveliness; thy bowering vines,
And glens of leafy shade - whose verdant screens,
Echo the wild bees hum, and warbled note,
Waft in cadence low, from the bulbul's heaven tuned throat.
And when oppressed by thirst the lurid air
Mocks suffering with show of succour near,
Stamping the mirage with the landscape fair
Amidst the phantoms of the desert drear;
Thy diamond streams on my parched eye will flash,
And memory's tortured ear, hear thy bright waters dash"

26 November 1839

Reluctantly we left Suadea. Luckily, Mr Barker, who was also going to Antakia, suggested we go back by a different and much more interesting route along the banks of the Orontes River, the views on which are very picturesque as it winds its way to the sea through the opening mountains. We crossed the river in a boat, and stopped to take some refreshment at the country house belonging to a resident of Antioch, well situated for enjoying the beauties of the surrounding scenery.

In this Valley I first saw the Cornubia tree, or Karub. This tree, with its dark green foliage, resembles the evergreen oak and bears a broad pod, full of saccharine matter, which when dry forms a nutritious condiment. It is called St John's bread. It's also called Locusta, and is reputed to be the locust on which St John fed. I was often reduced to this myself when unable to procure other food, carrying it in my saddlebags. The true Locust is also an article of food in these Eastern countries, and only available at uncertain times. It forms a major article of trade, being sold in all the shops in Turkey and Syria.

There's a great variety of the oak in the mountains of Amanus, but they do not grow to any size, and it would be worth the experiment to transplant some of these to more northern climates. The peasants in these hills use a small rock plant, which grows on their cliffs, as a substitute for quinine in cases of intermittent fever. It's a creeping plant of a dusty white appearance, possessing a fine aromatic bitter, and has been used with great success.

Continuing our route, we came to the spot which has been fixed on as the site of Daphne. Here a great number of copious springs gush from the downhill slide of a rocky hill. These have been conducted via small canals to a number of watermills, which in turn, supply Antioch with flour. When released from their work, rush down in innumerable shoots and miniature falls, entering a gully that conducts their free waters to the Orantes River. We were shown a raised ground plan of a building, said to be that of the temple, and a man brought us a small marble head of a lion, which he stated he had found here. But where are the Groves so celebrated? If they were destroyed wilfully, some few would have escaped to tell the tale, or others would have sprung from the seed or roots of their precursors? Now, not a tree spreads its shade to shelter the wayfarer or guide the antiquary.

Near the town we passed the large massive barracks built from the walls of Antioch. This, however, is incapable of holding all the troops collected here. Daily, troops are arriving and their miserable encampments cover all the open spots around the town, the officers alone having small tents, and the men's shelter consisting of cloths or felts supported on staves or poles. When the workmen were excavating the walls, they discovered a marble statue or bust, with a Latin inscription on the pilaster, which formed the continuation of the bust. This is now in the possesion of Mr E Barker, to whom Ibrahim Pasha, who was on the spot at the time, presented it, remarking "We English set a value on these things". The head of the statue is well executed and very perfect, with large Roman features and very little hair. The vaunting inscription informs us that this was "A man of men, whose celebrity was so great that it was not necessary to mention his name for him to be known," etc. So much for fame!

We rode from Antakia on 29th November, through the ruins of the old gates, the mountains rising in rocky crags on the right. These are full of excavations, amongst which my companion discovered a colossal Sphinx, though much effaced. We had a pleasant fellow traveller in a French officer in the Pasha's service, a nephew of Arago, the French savant (learned scholar). Travelling easterly over the plains we came to Kerim, at the foot of the mountains, which form the high land on which Aleppo is situated. Kerim is an artificial mound coated with stone, on the top of which are the ruins of a Saracen fortress. It is completely commanded by the adjacent hills, lying in a gorge. We found here only ruined houses, and one or two peasants, who remained for the sake of the watermills, of which there were several here. They informed us that the people had all left for a village on top of the hills, where they remained during the winter. There was abundance of water in springs, and at the foot of the mound was a warm spring, with a temperature of 80°. It took us an hour to climb to the top of the mountain, by a precipitous breakneck road, guided by one of the millers. Here we found a large village, apparently in a prosperous state and full of people. A rather extraordinary circumstance in this country with its present rulers!

Arago's Egyptian uniform insured us good accommodation in the sheik's house, where we made ourselves at home, although we had to keep up a blood feud with the fleas, who pleaded numbers and the right of prior occupation. From here there are two roads to Aleppo, one direct, but very bad, continuing across the hills; the other, the road we had left in the plain the previous evening, is longer, but not so rugged. Preferring the latter, we descended by the way we came, and resumed our journey through the plains, gradually ascending as we entered the hills. These hills have a brown barren appearance, and many of them are crowned with ugly ruins of walls and doorways. In the gorges were patches of trees, which relieve the sterility of the countryside. We reached Dana, a large village with some cultivation, in around six hours. We ought to have stopped over, but having rested and refreshed our horses, we pushed on for Tukaat, which took us another five hours. This place (also called Engeel, from its abounding in figs) we reached at nightfall by bad and rocky roads. We entered the streets of this large village to find rest after our long ride, but everything was silent. We explored some of the houses by the receding twilight, but they presented nothing but bare walls - the village was abandoned. The silence of the desert is grand and elevating, the silence of the grave in the solitary cemetery is impressive, but the silence of the deserted dwellings of man is gloomy and painful. A stray cow, which had sought shelter in the village, was a relief to our feeling of desolation to go on in search of more comfortable accommodation.

The night was very dark, and the road rocky and we had some difficulty in keeping on the track. We kept a sharp lookout for distant lights, and a sharp ear for the barking of some shepherd's dog, which could guide us to find a refuge for the night. Several times we made long excursions in pursuit of some activity and life which proved to be a rising star or the imaginary barking of dogs. It was simply the pulsation of our own overstrained hearing and eyesight in the darkness. In these cases, as it was not safe to abandon the track, which we would never have recovered. On one occasion, one of the party was detached on these wild goose chases, while the rest remained on the spot till his return, which was guided by the note of a bugle horn, which we blew at intervals, when we again resumed our weary ride. At length, after several hours, we heard the baying of dogs. This time we were certain, and we left the road in the direction of the welcome sound, sometimes lost by an intervening hill, or some other surmounting obstacle, until it we found ourselves in a large ruined village on rising ground. We first came to some large sheepfolds guarded by the dogs that had betrayed their retreat to us; and while we talked to the shepherd, we could see a number of dark figures against the clear western sky making their escape in different directions. We gave chase, in the hope of talking to them and in the process found an inhabited hovel by the light from around the door. Knocking on the door, some fine strapping fellows emerged from their concealment to protest against our violating their harem, which was confirmed by the alarmed voices of the woman within. It seems they took us for a party of Ibrahim Pasha's soldiers pressing men for the conscription, or robbing them of their property, and this accounted for the ruined and deserted villages so common in Syria. People abandoning their homes and flying to the wilds and deserts from the oppression of forever paying taxes.

Ibrahim Pasha has the reputation of being of a very sordid and miserly disposition, descending to the most degrading methods of making money. Amongst other things he speculated in pigs! But as this was an abomination enough to raise the Seven Sleepers (Companions of the Cave, is the story of a group of youths who hid inside a cave outside the city of Ephesus to escape religious persecution), and shock Muslim prejudices - he chose keep his herds of swine on the Christian tenant farms of the districts of Antioch, to be fed and returned to him in full tale when required, compelling them to make good any deficiency by death or accident. In like manner he forces the peasants to take so many yoke of his oxen for their agriculture - whether they require them or not… exacting his share of the produce as remuneration, besides having his cattle fed and returned after the season.

However, as our emergency was pressing, partly by assurances and partly by threats, we induced our friends to show us some place of accommodation. They first tried to lodge us in caves and ruins, but fearing we should take forcible possession of the harem, they at length conducted us to a large ruined building with a strong door in the lower part of it. After discussion with the inmates, some heavy bolts and bars were withdrawn, and we found ourselves in a comfortable room, surrounded by large jars of grain, butter, oil, etc, and occupied by a respectable old Muslim and his daughter. As soon the old man's alarm had subsided, he set about satisfying our craving appetites, whilst his daughter made bread on the hearth, and we fared much better than we had expected. Our host the next morning did not object, any more than the Sheik at Kerim, to being well paid for his hospitality

30 November 1839

In three hours we came in sight of Aleppo, which presents a lovely view on approach, with its numerous stone built mosques and minarets, and a high artificial mound in the centre, surmounted by the walls and gateways of the citadel. It is situated amongst barren rocky slopes, except where tracks of gardens and fruit orchards have been rescued by the copious supply of water for irrigation from the otherwise barren country. The olive and fig are cultivated here as well as the pistachio, and I am assured this is the only place in Syria where the latter grows. It has the appearance and size of a small leaved apple tree.

As experienced, it's always more difficult to find lodgings in towns and cities, than in villages. Here is an excellent example. We first went to the house of the British Consular agent, Mr Werry, a spacious and luxurious building, with reservoirs of water shaded by trees in the central court. On applying to his functionary for assistance, he sent one of his servants to conduct us to a khan, this was bad enough. After traversing the streets and bazaars of the town through its entire length, we discovered that we had not been sent to a respectable lodging. It was fortunate we did not remain there, as we afterwards found out that this khan was a gambling house, frequented by all the low and disreputable travellers of all nations in the place. Remanding Mr Werry's servant to his employer, we proceeded to the house of Mr Charles Barker, another son of Mr Barker of Suadea, who resides in a suburb of the town, which we passed on our entrance. This quarter is called the Katab, and is composed of wooden houses, with rooms on the ground floor only, for fear of earthquakes. It is inhabited by Europeans and Levantine Christians, who abandoned the city in consequence of an earthquake which happened three years previously and ruined a great part of Aleppo. Mr Barker, with the same kindness and hospitality we experienced from the rest of his family, received us into his house and accommodated us during our stay.

The city of Aleppo is the best built of any in the Turkish dominions, the numerous elegant mosques, houses, and arched bazaars being all built of hewn stone beautifully put together. One house I visited was remarkably handsome, the sides of the square surrounding the courtyard being ornamented with projecting Gothic roofs, which, as well as the ceilings of the rooms, were covered with arabesque painting and gilding, that in the rooms being executed with much taste. Under this house we descended three stories of vaults, cut from the solid rock, the materials from which we were told had been used in the building.

The bazaars are crowded with people, and have a very colorful appearance, the Aleppines being celebrated for their finery in dress. This place, unlike Stamboul, is essentially an eastern city, our costume being seen only on Europeans: the Muslims are partial to gaudy colours, wearing green, white, or striped turbans. The Syrian Christians, of whom there are around 15,000 here, wear flowing dresses and large grey turbans, and mixing with these are the Arabs in their broad striped abbaes and bright yellow kefiehs with long scarlet fringe, besides a number of Persians in their uncouth attire. These latter form part of a caravan of pilgrims on its way to Mecca in Saudi Arabia and Karbala in Iraq.

Passing through the long bazaars, the shops of which are hung with shawls and scarves, shoes of all colours, swords and arms, etc, you come to open space surrounded by ruins, with the exception of some elegant mosques. In this place the horse market is held, which is a lively scene and worth witnessing. The horse "dellels," or brokers, are a shrewd lot of fellows, equally expert at fleecing both buyers and sellers: they wear scarlet cloaks lined with fur, large coloured turbans, long boots, swords and pistols. Wherever there is a smooth, less crowed spot, they are galloping the horses entrusted to them to dispose of. Apart from the crowds, groups are collected on the different mounds discussing the merits or value of mules, pack horses or camels. Here and there a wary Arab, leading a blood looking horse, ornamented with coloured tassels and fringes passes a number of booths, where the country people are selling tobacco and other produce, fruit, flowers and poultry. On the right rises the mound, on the summit of which is the citadel, a gateway and bridge crossing the moat, and an ascent of steps leading up to the walls. The Christians of Aleppo were in great consternation least they should be included in the conscription, the Egyptian government having contemplated embodying them as militia, to which they have an utter aversion. If they were employed merely on the spot, it would be of great advantage to them to be armed, even for their own protection, as the hatred of the Turks, or mixed population of Aleppo, towards the Christians, is so strong that it was confidently believed that had Ibrahim Pasha been vanquished at the battle of Nezib, there would have been a general massacre of all the Christians in the city. If they were armed, they might protect themselves – that is, if they had the spirit to defend their own, which is doubtful.

I was told here by a Greek priest that the scriptures as possessed by the Armenians, Catholics, Greeks and Maronites were all alike, but their differences arose from their following the commentaries of the chiefs of their several sects. This is much the case nearer home! The French Society of Aleppo is composed of consular agents, merchants and European instructors in the Egyptian service. I had an opportunity of attending some of the evening reunions, which were interesting from their novelty. The ladies, some of whom are very good looking, all wore the Syrian costume, silk trousers and a frock in three pieces, that is, split vertically, a long embroidered jacket of coloured cloth or velvet, and a rich shawl sash. The headdress is a small coloured turban festooned with seed pearl, the hair plaited in long braids and hung with gold coins, necklaces of which ornament the neck. This dress is handsome and luxurious, but requires a fine person to make it look graceful. They all sat cross-legged or reclined on the divans around the walls, never moving except to dance, after which they resumed their places. Conversation was out of the question, except among themselves: however, the gentleman indemnified themselves on their side for their taciturnity by smoking long cherry stick pipes and narghilehs, till the room was so clouded with smoke that it was difficult to see across it, while one of the host's family was going round with a bag of prime Latakia to replenish the exhausted pipes of the smokers. This was rendered more absurd by the gentleman wearing the European dress, with the exception of a red fez, and sitting on chairs. Some of the elderly ladies smoked narghilehs, and the younger ones would have had no objection, but were fearful it might deduct from their youthful status.

The weather is becoming colder by the day, and we are threatened with a rainy and unpleasant ride, besides hearing reports of the roads being unsafe - I believe the country is nearly cleared of petty robbers by the wholesale Egyptian bandits. I heard a good story of an English traveller who was walking with a friend in Aleppo, when he was saluted by an Italian, who congratulated him on his safe arrival. The Englishman, instead of returning his salutation, abused him in no measured terms, notwithstanding the remonstrances of the man, who, thinking him gone crazy, quickly made his exit. On his friend enquiring how the man had deserved this treatment, "Why, said he, the rascal was the cause of my being robbed - I met him at Latakia, when he advised me to use the road via Antioch, as the direct road was unsafe, and as it is a rule I always follow exactly the opposite road from what I am recommended. I travelled via the direct route and was attacked and stripped"! However, the principal was not bad: where there is an active government in the country, a road on which one robbery has been committed may generally be considered safe, as the perpetrators in fear of being arrested will have made their escape, or gone to another part of the country.

I was informed that between Aleppo and Palmyra there is a sub-tribe of Arabs living amongst the Anazee tribes, who subsist entirely by hunting the gazelle. They are called Sleibe or gypsies. They live on the flesh of these animals, and their clothes and tents are made from the skins. Their mode of taking the gazelle is odd. When they have found a place frequented by them, an extensive tunnel wall is constructed, gradually narrowing to an angle, at which point it is partially broken down, and a deep ditch dug on the other side. The herd is then surrounded, and naturally presses to the widest opening to escape, when the Arabs close in and pursue them down the tunnel, where, finding no other outlet, they leap the broken wall and fall into the pit on the other side.

The natives of Aleppo are a handsome race, and even to the lowest classes are polite and obliging. I had little opportunity of seeing their women folk, but should suppose they were equally so. I cannot say much for the beauty of the Levantine ladies, who have sharp unmeaning faces, with some few exceptions, and these were very lovely. When a stranger calls at their houses, it is the ladies duty to present him with coffee and they pride themselves on being good cooks, notwithstanding their affectation of European refinement. The servants are generally poor relations of the family, who of course do not feel the degradation, as the wife is little more than a head servant. It is a system of mutual accommodation, and a remnant of patriarchal customs.

The belief in the power of the evil eye is very strong here among the Muslims and Christians, and their dread of it commensurate. For this reason, they purposely avoid ornamenting their children, and even washing them, for fear of the envy or evil eye of their neighbours, imagining it can create illness and other bad effects. They are never at a loss for a variety of instances of persons who have been thus smitten, entirely overlooking the majority who have remained unharmed, but whose mishaps, if they had happened, would have been attributed to this cause. If you enquire what ails a sick person, he replies "Oh, it's only people's eyes"! And it is very remarkable how extended this superstition has always been, so that it gives grounds to imagine that it has some foundation in truth.

As it is stronger in Ireland than England, it may have been introduced into that country by the Carthaginians, and come to England from there, or else it may have been introduced direct by the Phoenicians, if, indeed, it was not indigenous. For example, in England, if you offer a man a price for a horse, he expects it will fall lame, or something else will happen to it. Amongst the Arabs this feeling is so strong that a man will seldom venture to keep a horse that has been put a price on, and he has been pressed to part with. In Ireland, it is the custom on entering a place where any occupation is going on to say, "God bless the work", and you cannot offend a mother more than by praising her child without saying "God bless it!" In the same way, amongst the Moors, it is considered a great insult to admire a horse or anything belonging to them, and not add this qualification. Amongst the Barbary Jews nothing gives more offence to a pretty girl than to extol her beauty without praising God for it, or to commend their children without blessing them. In fact, it is looked on as a piece of gratuitous malice, and is generally met with some exclamation equivalent to "May the omen be averted!". To counteract the effects of this dreaded evil eye, their children's dresses are embroidered with figures of hands, and five fingers are painted on their doorposts and furniture, the number five being considered a powerful charm against its influence. Virgil has, "Nescio quis teneros oculos mihi fascinate agnos," and the remarks of the great Lord Bacon also pertinent and extraordinary, that I cannot help inserting some of them here - "There be none of the affections which have been noted to fascinate or bewitch, but love and envy: they both have vehement wishes: they frame themselves readily into imaginations and suggestions, and they come easily into the eye, especially upon the presence of the objects which are the points that conduce to fascination, if any such thing be…. so that still there seemeth to be acknowledged in the act of envy an ejaculation or irradiation of the eye: nay, some have been so curious as to note that the times when the stroke or percussion of an envious eye doth most hurt, are, when the party envied is beheld in glory or triumph: for that sets an edge upon envy: and besides at such times the spirits of the person envied to come forth most into the outward parts, and so meet the blow".

The people of Aleppo and Aintab are subject to a most afflicting disease, which they call "the Aleppo boil". It is not peculiar to the natives, as strangers are said invariably to be attacked with it after a week's residence; however, it appears there are exceptions, as I was there a month without being infected. It generally attacks the face, but often the arms, feet, and other parts of the body, beginning with a red swelling, which increases and spreads till it often penetrates to the bone, sometimes carrying away the nose, and always leaving most ungainly scars: infants are not exempted from this scourge, and I have seen ladies' faces quite seamed with the marks of it. I should advise no lady, who has any regard for her beauty, to visit Aleppo. No remedy has been found to check the progress of this afflicting disease by the medical practitioners of the Pasha's troops, who themselves suffer much from it, except cauterizing it, which also leaves a scar, besides the danger of performing it. No origin or cause has been found for it except that, attributed to most local maladies and infections - that it is caused by the water. I afterwards found this infection at Baghdad, where I was told it was caused by eating dates, and consequently called the "Date mark". It has the same features as at Aleppo, and was as common. Although they consume dates at the latter place, they do not grow there. However, I have no doubt, if enquiry were made, this peculiar complaint would be found to extend over the whole course of the Euphrates River, and may arise from some mineralogical pollution of the water, or some minute insect which inhabits it.

The Aleppines are fond of hunting and they have two sorts of greyhounds. The common Persian black, with feathered tail, and a stronger greyhound with smooth hair, fawn coloured, with black muzzle. They take the gazelle with the assistance of the goshawk, which confuses the animal by striking at its head. I saw a greyhound stolen in a very clever way in the open street. A well-dressed horseman was riding in, leading his favourite dog by a rope, when a boy ran behind him, unfastened the cord from the greyhounds' collar, and tied it to the horse's tail. He never took his eyes off the man until he had secured his prize, and the horseman jogged on, rope in hand, quite innocent of his loss. He only discovered this towards the end of the street, and, I believe, managed to recover his dog. It was a remarkably clever trick, and showed how ingenious the rascal was.

The River of Aleppo produces two species of fish, which are much enjoyed; the one is like a minnow, but flatter; the other a short greenish black mud fish, which does not look tempting. This stream is lost in a marshy lake, about forty miles south of the town; and I am told that the village at the spot, called Kinesrin, the site of Chalcis, is inhabited by fire worshippers, and I hear of others to the north. The vegetation along the river is teaming with woodcocks.

The Jebel Anzeyry, a range of mountains running north and south through Syria to join the Anti Lebanon, is inhabited by an extraordinary race of people, of whom little is known. They are swarthy, with a downcast suspicious look, and are supposed to be worshippers of idol gods. They say that they are prohibited from eating pork, and are bound to stab any Christian that may walk before them. However, at present they dare not follow this precept. I should think a visit to their country would be interesting. They may be a remnant of the ancient idol worshippers of Syria.

The large transit commerce, which formally came from the East through Aleppo, is now extinct. There is at present a good trade carried on in raw silk, as also in European goods, printed cotton shawls, handkerchiefs, etc, and a large caravan arrives now and then from Baghdad with Shiraz tobacco, called Tumbuk, for which the traders exchange the striped silk fabrics of Aleppo.

This fine city was very much damaged by the last earthquake, which destroyed many of the houses and mosques, and some of the minarets at present standing are very much out of the perpendicular. It is very common to see these leaning towers in other parts of Turkey, particularly in Roumelia, either from this cause or from the foundations having given away.

Our direct route lay through Mesopotamia (Iraq) to Persia (Iran); but being so near Syria and Palestine, the temptation to visit these countries was too great to be resisted, and we accordingly diverged from our course for that purpose. Yet, writing after its accomplishment, of all the imaginable wretched and miserable undertakings which experience has realised or imagination pictured, nothing can equal in discomfort a winter journey in Syria, combining rain, or rather water en masse, mud up to the horses girths, intense cold, nothing to eat, no shelter at night except to be devoured by fleas, altogether such a concatenation of horrors as could only have been experienced by Baillie Fraser (A Winters Journey in Persia by Fraser), or dreamt of by those who never underwent the ordeal. After seeing the localities, I can well understand why the disciples were told to pray that their flight might not be in the winter. Sometimes the roads are quite impassable, at least to emigrants with families, but, thank God, we at length safely reached the spot where the holy city once stood.

8 December 1839

Leaving Aleppo, we went south west over rocky undulating plains, remarkable for nothing but large flocks of buzzards and gazelles feeding by the roadside. The weather was cold. We passed the village of Kan Tuman, and arrived at Sermein after a nine hour ride. Here our accommodation was very bad. We lodged in a room without doors, and were not sorry to leave at an early hour, travelling south over the same plains, which became less stony as we advanced. At the village of Khaneh Sibl, we met a squadron of Lancers of the Egyptian army, marching north. There was about 2000 of them. The men were lightly but neatly armed and dressed, and the horses were very superior and in excellent condition. This is the only situation for which Ibrahim Pasha will go to any expense. Although he may compel the natives to sell their horses, he always gives them their full value. At this village we wished to water our horses; but with some of the soldiers being near, the villagers told us that there was no water to be had and what water was being used was bought from a long distance. However, they presently gave us a hint that if we waited till the troops were gone, we might be served. Accordingly when they had filed off, we were taken to a well of good water, which had been concealed by brambles on the approach of the troops.

The weather is showery, which is a prelude to the winter rains. We passed several ruins of mud walls, which had been villages, and reached Marrah, after a seven hour ride. We did not enter this place. It looked large and ruinous, and contains a new cavalry barrack. A great many of the troops were drawing water at a well outside the gates by means of long rope over a pulley drawn by a donkey down an inclined plane and the men appeared civil. As there was no village on the road between this and Shokune, we diverged eastwards and about five miles further, came to a community of people who were living in caves underground, probably inhabitants of some of the deserted villages.

After another two hours we came to the semi-deserted village of Kiffoor-bashi, where we took possession of the sheik's house, after first expelling three camels. In their places we stabled our horses, which were divided from us by low wall. We found our system of not carrying provisions very near akin to starvation in this wretched country. At times we could not even procure burgool (wheat that has been steamed or parboiled, dried and ground requiring little preparation). At a village further on I had an illustration of scripture history. I asked for milk and was told they had none. I said I'd seen a herd of cattle coming in as I arrived. "Oh, said the man, you would not drink cow's milk and we have no sheep". Sheep are regularly milked in these countries, and cows' milk is never used except sour.

10 December 1839

From here it was a four hour ride to Khan Shokune, across plains of fine red soil, on which, from the few days of rain, the grass was fast springing up. This is a large village at the foot of an artificial mound. It has a stone built mosque and khan furnished with baths. In front of it are two large square reservoirs of water with a peculiar appearance on approaching it, as the houses are all formed like sugar loaves of light coloured mud. We continued our route across the plains without a break, with a view to the distant ridge of Jebel Anzirie in the West, varied with flights of lapwings and jackdaws, and immense numbers of larks. This country, which extends to Palmyra, if one may credit the report of the natives, is very fertile, and capable of much cultivation. It formally supported a large population evidenced from the numerous artificial mounds spread over its level surface, each of which indicates the site of a town.

We passed a village on the left on a mound called Taiba, and another, a little further on, both of them built in the same conical style. Descending by winding gullies to the valley of the Orontes River, we came to Hamah, after a five hour ride. The view of Hamah is fine, nearly as large as Aleppo, and backed by high cliffs. These cliffs are full of caves and excavations, inhabited by local tribes.

The Orantes River flows through the centre of the town, bordered with trees, and washing the foot of a high artificial mound which arises from amongst the houses on its banks. It is covered with grass, from the moisture rising from the river, and is about 200 yards in length. This place must be very beautiful in the summer, the houses being interspersed with trees in groves lining the banks of the Orontes River. The houses are roofed with domes and arches, on account of the scarcity of timber for building. The waterwheels for supplying the town are, I suppose, the largest known. These enormous wheels are worked entirely by the current, and discharge their water into aqueducts, supported on two or more tiers of arches. These aqueducts and dripping wheels are very picturesque, as well as the houses which run up in groups, in range above range, halfway up to the cliffs.

We crossed the river, and entered the town through the crowded, dirty, and uncovered bazaars, and made our way to the chief's house, who sent a man to find us accommodation. This took a search of the whole town and at last we were accommodated in a miserable house in the upper town, already occupied by a man and his wife, and full of stores, part of which were dislodged to make room for us. We were too tired to return and complain of our treatment, or find a better lodging, so we submitted with resignation, and as the owners seemed inclined to please us, we lay down on our carpets. We were compelled to witness that never-ought-to-be-seen process of cooking, which went far towards blunting our keen appetites. The unlikely casserole, containing our anticipated mess, was most precariously situated between a litter of half naked children, is black and dirty as young buffaloes, and a woman very little cleaner, who was alternately employed superintending cookery and feeding these bantlings according to their ages. At night we were eaten by fleas, besides being haunted by cats, who seemed to think our heads excellent landing places on which to alight when jumping down from the bags and boxes above us.

The natives of Hamah have a very Jewish physiognomy, and are extremely bigoted and fanatical. Ibrahim Pasha finds it difficult to keep them quiet, and a troop of artillery arrived here today to check their unruliness.

There are no Jews at Hamah, as there is a long running feud between the Moslems, according to the following account, which is well authenticated. About 10 years ago the Jews of Hamah, having a dispute with the native Christians, devised a plan of revenge, which, however, recoiled on them. They employed an Arab to shoot a wild hog and the head of which was thrown into the fountain of the principal mosque at night, where the Turks performed their ablutions before the Namaz. The next morning, of course, there was a general consternation amongst the true believers, who were horrified at discovering the head of the unclean beast in their very sanctuary. They vowed vengeance against the perpetrators of this sacrilege, and they did not want Jews, stationed for the purpose, who suggested that no suspicion could fall on their race, who held the animal in the same detestation as themselves. The public rage was then directed towards the Christian population, and the fermentation was on the point of ending in a general massacre of the professors of that faith. Fortunately, at this critical moment, the Arab who had supplied the pork, not having left the town, and hearing the cause of the tumult, came forward and offered to point out the man to whom he had sold it. He proved to be a Jew, and was brought before the chief and foot wipped (bastinadoed). A full confession was extorted and he was then executed. The fury of the mob being allayed, the rest of the tribe were banished from the place, where they dare not return on peril of their lives. I was even advised to cut my hair, lest I should be taken for a Jew, as they all have the sides of their heads unshaven, while the Moslems shave the whole head.

The women of Hamah are muffled up in a large wrapper, concealing every part of the face but the eyes. Over the nose is suspended a small gold cylinder, from which hang several gold coins of different sizes and their earrings are very heavy, and suspended over the upper part of the ear.

Hamah was called by the Greeks, Epiphania. If this be the Hamath of scripture, it would seem that the Hebrews never occupied the whole of the promised land. After the partition there remained yet very much land to be possessed, amongst which is enumerated "All Lebanon toward the sun rising from Baal Gad under mount Hermon, to the entering in of Hamath" (Joshua xiii 5). This does not militate against the former prophecies, for in the prospective prophecy of Ezekiel (xlvii 20) the same is repeated in defining the boundaries of the land. "The west side shall be the great sea from the border till a man come over against Hamath". This line would reach the sea between Tortosa and Aradus, and include the whole of Lebanon, a very small portion of which was within the ancient limits of Palestine.

Although in the time of David the whole of Syria was subdued, it was only rendered tributary, and not incorporated in the possessions of the tribes: and Solomon's dominion, in like manner, extended to the Euphrates, as was promised to Abraham.

11 December 1839

We travelled onwards across the plains which were becoming heavy with rain. This road seems to be much frequented by traders between Damascus and Aleppo, but the principal people we met were Arabs, with black striped cloaks, carrying long guns or spears, from the tops of which hung tufts of black ostrich feathers: they generally rode mares, not remarkable for beauty; there were a few, however, which would have brought a high price anywhere.

After a four hour ride we came to Rostan, a large walled village of some 400 houses, on the precipitous hills forming the bank of the Orontes River. This place had a very picturesque appearance and is surrounded by black stone walls, and the river is crossed by a handsome bridge of black-and-white stone of eleven arches. Just below this bridge the water falls in cascades over the bed of the river, where it is conducted to flour mills. The Lebanon Mountains are on the west, capped with snow. A roomy khan stands on the opposite side. The Orontes River traverses these plains in a deep narrow gully, and are never seen till you come to the verge of the descent. Ascending a ravine full of artificial looking conical rocks and peaks of sandstone, we came in full sight of the snow caps of Lebanon. We passed the village of Tellé and reached Homs in five hours from Rostan.

The horses we had brought from Istanbul, gave in. We were obliged to send them to the market and dispose of them for what they would bring, as their backs were much galled, from the heavy Turkish saddles, which were not off their backs for eight, ten, and sometimes twelve hours a day. However, it was due to our neglecting the advice of the Arabs, never to unsaddle our horses at night during a journey. The weather had become so cold that immediately their backs were uncovered they rose in swellings wherever the saddles had pressed, even after allowing them an hour to cool, and these swellings were rubbed into sores when the saddles were replaced. I afterwards benefited by this advice, and found that after keeping the saddle on for thirty days my horse's back was sound. Our horses sold for less than half their cost, but they had done us good service, and we were told we could always procure hired cattle to the south, which is preferable in bad weather. However, in fine weather it is by far the most advantageous plan to ride your own horses.

We were accommodated in the house of the sheik of the Christians, who is the responsible head of the denomination for the time his office lasts. His job is to settle the market prices, collect contributions and assessments, and billet travellers, fleecing his people as much as possible, knowing that he too, in turn, will be squeezed by his chief. According to Eastern rules he may be a winner, but he holds no sinecure.

The house, each room of which contained a family, was full of woman and children all dressed in dirty blue rags, and squalling and screaming from morning till night. Some of them had fevers, and I'm only astonished they are not visited with the plague, due to the filthy state of the town and there and unclean habits. In addition, this house has a large pool of stagnant water in the centre of the courtyard. It is very trying being detained in such places, but as the weather is very rainy, we consider ourselves fortunate in having a shelter of any sort.

Homs, formerly Hemessa (probably originally from Greek) is an extensive town, built of stone, with an immense artificial mound of white earth on its south side. Of the Acropolis which crowned this hill little now remains. The hill itself is decaying and being washed away by the action of the rains. This place is in a fine situation, commanding a prospect of the mountains in the east; on that side also lies an extensive lake, called by the natives Eskeli. The town contains some covered bazaars and several large khans and one of Ibrahim Pasha's new barracks, where corps of artillery are stationed, consisting of 36 pieces and around 2000 men. The number of families that pay the poll tax or ferdi at Homs is 5800, on which 4500 are Turks and 1300 Christians; which, reckoning five persons to each family on an average, would give a population of around 29,000. There are no Jews here.

The people of the towns and villages of Syria and Palestine have been deprived of their arms by the Egyptian government, either voluntarily or by compulsion. This is a very political measure with a turbulent people, as long as it is not made to minister to oppression.

In these towns are to be found a great many coins and antique intaglios (engraving or incision in stone or other hard material) which are brought from Balbec, Palmyra and other mines of antiquity. The best places to procure them are the shops in the jewellers' bazaars, where the Arabs dispose of the silver and gold coins for their weight to be melted down. The goldsmiths, knowing their value, generally preserve them and purchase the antiques for a trifle, awaiting an opportunity of disposing of them again to Europeans, which on this line of road does not often occur. We used to amuse ourselves at the shops by examining the curious medley contained in the little cabinets in which they kept the materials of their trade. They consisted of a great variety of cut glass jewels of all colours, sets of stones, agates and coloured beads, and a few amethysts, turquoises and garnets of little value.

Amongst these are generally found copper and silver coins, intaglios, cameos and engraved stones. Many spoilt by the friction of the years in such hard company, some broken and but few perfect. The antique intaglios are commonly executed on white or red cornelian. We procured a few of these, and I might have bought many more; but, with such a long and precarious journey before me, did not like to encumber myself with anything worth losing. The inscribed stones were very numerous, most of them with Cufic inscriptions. Very good Greek and Roman silver and copper coins can be obtained here. We saw a few of gold of some of the Roman emperors. One of these was a rare copper coin of Corycus in Cilicia, with turreted head, and, on the reverse, a Mercury. Another coin was of Antiochus, King of Syria, BC 145. Besides coins of Antoninus, Gallienus, Faustina, and many Christian coins, with figures with sceptre and halo, and inscribed Christus Basilius Basilii.

There are very expert at making false coins, and it requires a great deal of discrimination to avoid being imposed upon, for the mould is taken from a good coin. An Armenian, who was much inclined, but not clever enough, to be a rogue, brought us a very fine Alexander coin for sale, but, fortunately, before striking the bargain, seeing we were pleased with it, he said he had several more which he would dispose of on the same terms. He went away and shortly returned with seven or eight more, all evidently cast in the same die, which, on further examination, proved to be fake, and of no value except as facsimiles. They were not even made with pure silver.

The variety of dialects of the Arabic language in use in the Middle East is very remarkable, and, though I had acquired the dialect spoken around Morocco, I found this of very little use in Syria, until I became accustomed to the language of the different places we came to, and with time could master the various dialects spoken. At Damascus, Homs, Hamah, Aleppo, and Jerusalem, Arabic is spoken; but each place has its peculiar dialect, likewise in Baghdad, Egypt, and the several Barbary states; but the Arabic of the Koran is a dormant language, and has the same relation to the others as Latin has to Italian, French, and Spanish. Even Maltese is an Arab dialect. I heard of a professor of Arabic from Denmark (Prof. Vonhaven) going on a scientific mission to Egypt, and not being able to understand a word of the language spoken by the natives.

As the road not being much travelled, we experienced more difficulty than we had anticipated in procuring horses or mules for hire, and were compelled to apply to the governor of the place for assistance, who very ungraciously refused to help us. From his disobliging behaviour, coupled with the meanness of his appearance, he certainly could not have been an

Osmanli. We found ourselves in a dilemma. We could only procure donkeys or camels, and the owners refused to go on any other road other than to Tripoli or Damascus and we began to regret parting with our horses. As the road to Beirut was impassable from mud and snow on the mountains, we had no option but to continue the trip on donkeys to Tripoli. Camels were out of the equation as they are very dangerous along wet roads, where they can't keep their footing.

14 December 1839

When the donkeys were bought, they proved much better than we had expected, being large and powerful, and the size of ponies. Dividing our baggage among the three, we rode out of the town, taking an easterly route, through oceans of mud, into which, as we were not yet accustomed to riding these new animals, we every now and then slipped off, although we had loops of rope to serve as stirrups. These only encumbered our falls, and, notwithstanding our vexation, we could not help laughing at the ludicrous scenes and the ungainly appearance we exhibited before we had travelled many miles, covered in mud!.

Our road led over a stony plain passing north of the Lake of Homs, the shores of which are not higher than the surrounding level, and soon after we ascended the hills. This is a very gradual and easy pass to Tripoli, between what would seem the southern termination of the Jebel Ansiri and the north of the Lebanon. Crossing over this ridge, we opened the valley of Lebanon on our left, riding in wooded gullies on either side until they met in the distant perspective: their tops already whitening under the hand of December. We passed a village called Heddedee, composed of black stone hovels, the materials for which seemed to have been gathered from a neighbouring mound of ruins.

Further on we reached a similar group of huts, called Nasee, and as there was no other shelter within a reasonable distance, we stopped here for the night, after eight hours slow riding. To the north rose a commanding bluff mountain – spur, covered with the picturesque fortress of Kalat el Hosn, flooded with light from the setting sun, and relieved by a background of black stormy clouds, the contents of which were not long in descending in torrents to the earth. Our lodging was most miserable. A large fire in the middle of the hovel filled it with dense smoke, and to avoid suffocation we were obliged to lie on the ground, to be within the draft of the fire. This, of course, exposed us all the more to the attacks of fleas, but, listening to the rain and storm without, we made ourselves happy by comparison. Even here we found some regulars impressing recruits for the army.

15 December 1839

The morning broke clear and cloudless. We ascended the mountains, leaving Kalat el Hosn on the right, mingling its outline with the wooded crags. This castle was garrisoned by the Crusaders during their occupation. The water had run off the slopes, leaving the track more passable then we could have anticipated. We passed through a small valley with a few huts called Ain el Haramia (The well of the robbers), and continued over the mountains, which were covered with verdure, through woods of Ilex (a type of oak). Here we roused a huge wild boar, which cantered off unscathed, as we did not expect such large game. Soon afterwards three wolves crossed our path, pursued by number of shepherds' dogs. We stopped to speak to these shepherds, and obtained some milk, which they readily gave us, but refused to be paid, a very remarkable trait to meet with in Syria.

In the afternoon the weather becoming threatening, we were forced to look out for cover - but all the villages we came to were deserted. At length, descending from the mountains towards the coast, we made for a village about two miles off the road on the side of the hills. On reaching this by name of Telabas we find more evidence of Egyptian civilisation. There were no men in the place, and the women informed us that the day before, the governor of Tripoli, with a party of horsemen, had been there on a plundering excursion. On hearing them approach, all the men ran away to the mountains, to avoid paying their contributions, which are often levied several times from the same persons. Enraged at their disappointment, the governor ordered the women to be beaten, and then plundered the village of whatever he could find, so that we with difficulty obtained some eggs and sour milk. After eight hours riding we slept and left the next morning.

16 December 1839

We rode across the plain of Tripoli, feeling our way through the water with which it was submerged, and the track destroyed by the numerous streams from the mountains. Before we had proceeded 5 miles, the rain again came down in sheets, accompanied by a beating south-wester. It was with great difficulty we could make our unfortunate donkeys bear up. After some hard labour, we at length reached an old ruined khan. Here we found shelter, but could not succeed in making a fire for want of dry fuel. About 12 o'clock the weather cleared, and we once more started, wading through the mud, passing several villages at the foot of the mountains, along an atrocious road of water and stones, to the gates of Tripoli. A large and ancient looking town, strongly built of stone, with numerous streets and bazaars. It is celebrated for oranges and lemons, which are sent to Aleppo, Damascus and Jerusalem, as well as to other towns in Syria.

We proceeded to the house of our native consular agent, and were ushered into a handsome hall, in the form of a cross paved with marble, with a lofty dome over the centre. We amused ourselves while waiting for the owner's arrival, by examining the names carved on the walls. I was much impressed at finding the name of that talented and intrepid traveller, Davidson, who fell victim to his spirit of enterprise when crossing this Sahara, in an attempt to reach Timbuctoo. About this time four years ago I met him at Mogadore in Morocco, and was one of the last people to shake hands with him when he left the coast on his perilous and eventually fatal expedition. He had travelled in Egypt and Syria, where there was a settled government, with tents, baggage etc, and he thought he could do the same in the wilderness, where every man is his own master. From the account we received of his fate, it would appear that he was the victim of the jealousy of two chiefs. Poor Davidson had paid a large sum in dollars to a sheik of the Woled Abo-Sebah, who lived to the south of the Noon River, bordering the African desert, for protection through his country, and a promise to forward him across the desert through his friends. But the sheik of El Harib, a tribe who have a bad reputation even amongst the Arabs, and the same that endangered Caillie (a French explorer) on his return, wishing to injure his rival, and blacken his name of not being able to protect his guest for whose safety he had pledged, sent a party to intercept him, who treacherously shot him from behind, when he suspected no danger. A Jew servant and a freed Negro, whom he had bought from Jamaica, were spared; but his effects were all carried off.

I think it much more probable that the cupidity of the roving tribes was excited by the report of Davidson's wealth, from his spending lavishly whilst travelling in Morocco and paying so high for safe conduct. Imagining that he had much property with him, the sheik of El Harib attacked him for the sake of what he could steal, probably with the connivance of the sheik of Wed Noon, who would share the spoil, although it might have endangered his interests to have taken any active part in the affair. The sheik of Wed Noon is more within reach of the power of the Sultan, from the extensive commercial dealings of his tribesmen in the seaports of Morocco. However it is only an hypothesis, as the sheik bore a good character, but an Arab is like tamed leopard, you never know how far you can trust him; particularly with the certainty of impunity in a country where I myself was present. For example, where two respectable men were joking and laughing whilst settling, without any concealment, the share each should contribute of a sum of money (about $30), to be paid for having another man assassinated for a blood feud.

There are two ways of reaching the Niger from Morocco; one as a mendicant, which Caillie accomplished; the other by accompanying the regular caravan across the great desert as a merchant, when you are only exposed to the same risks from heat, etc, as others. I am convinced I could have visited Timbuctoo in this manner with the greatest ease: but from the accounts of the natives who had returned from it, there would appear little to repay the hardship and fatigues of the journey, except the satisfaction of being able to say, "I was there!". They describe it as a large extent of huts of wattle and mud, the only houses in the place belonging to the Moorish merchants who have settled there, for the sake of trade and built houses for themselves.

After this digression to the centre of Africa, retournons à Tripoli, where we remained for three days, until the rain had abated, enjoying the hospitality of the consul, who was a Levantine. The ladies wore the same dress as at Aleppo, but more overloaded with ornaments, the braided hair behind being matted with gold coins; some could not have had on less than £50 worth, besides pearls, etc.

The orange orchards are outside the town, but not perceivable till you come close to them, being sunk as it were in pits, so that the tops of the trees are level with the surrounding ground. There are numerous other gardens, and a long walk brings you to the harbour, where there is a small town called the Marina, composed of storehouses, counting houses, timber yards and a few shops. There were many great large fishing boats lying up on the beach, and others building, and numerous stone pillars were lying about, giving evidence of the fall of some place of greater antiquity. The promontory on which this échelle is built has been walled off, and fortified on the land side, and there are a great many ruins of walls and towers bordering the beach. From the Marina the view of Tripoli is splendid, seen across a fine placid sheet of water forming an inner bay. On the opposite side is a ruined castle on an island: a margin of reads and trees lines the shore beyond, above which rises the town, surmounted by a castle and the minarets of seven or eight mosques. Behind this rises the high straight ridge of Mount Lebanon, striated horizontally with snow. The situation of the town is very beautiful. Considerable trade is carried on here with Marseille and other Mediterranean ports.

19 December 1839

After some trouble with finding some horses we succeeded in getting pretty well mounted. We had not been two hours on the road, however, before the storms again commenced, and as the road wound along the coast, we had the benefit of an unimpeded gale, the rain beating horizontally. We passed Callimone on the coast, and Shik a Shika and several other villages on the heights to the left, which are inhabited by Maronites. At sunset, we crossed an abrupt rugged pass over a mountainous head land, the hills on either side rising in rocky terraces. After the descending the opposite slopes, whilst plunging through a slough of water and marsh, the moon suddenly emerged from a mass of black clouds, and revealed a most romantic scene. In the centre, between the jaws of a steep mountain gorge, rose abruptly a tall craggy pinnacle of rock crowned with a ruined castle; this picturesque building seemed to be a continuation of the rock on which it was built. Round its foot boiled a mountain torrent swollen by the rains, rushing under a narrow bridge without parapets. By moonlight, with black stormy heavens, the scene was wild and imposing. However, I did not experience so much pleasure in crossing the torrent, as in contemplating it as part of the view. The above-mentioned bridge would have answered the purpose of Al Sirat, but instead of being level, the two sides formed nearly a right angle, meeting at a point. Climbing over this by the uncertain light was nervous work; for it was not even wide enough for two to pass each other. This eyrie is called Kalat el M'selha. Soon afterwards we stopped at Batrone, six hours from Tripoli, and lodged in a long gloomy khan or tunnel on four massive arches. I slung my hammock across the corner of this gloomy vault, while the Greek, who filled the office of khanji, procured some fried eggs, and I made myself comparatively comfortable. One learns on these journeys how very little food a man can live on.

20 December 1839

Between here and Acre, the wayfarer passes a number of sheds and hovels, kept by Greeks, who, as he approaches, assail him with tempting inducements to halt, in the shape of fresh eggs, grilled fowls, pillaus, and other powerful sedatives, which, if he does not stop his ears, are likely to make him forget his day's ride. These places will also afford a shelter at night in case of necessity. The road today was stony, over the low cliffs by the seaside. On reaching Gebail, the ancient Byblus, I left the horses outside and walked through the town. It is surrounded with high dark walls and the interior is half in ruins and it's only street, full of mud. Some massive stone columns were strewed about among the ruins, and, finding nothing more of interest, I carried on. After crossing Nahr Ibrahim, a stream spanned by a single arch of great breadth and elegance with its upper walls and parapet broken away, nearly to the shell itself, giving it the appearance of great fragility, I found another small arch, which is only full during the floods. The banks of the stream are lined with trees and the rose laurel or oleander. Through the bridge the peaks and swells of the mountain are seen rising in rich luxuriance. The scenery improves here as the mountains approach the coast, but I was not long allowed to enjoy it, as the rain again came down in torrents. I was compelled to take shelter in one of the refreshment shops before mentioned from the fury of the storm. The sky having cleared off, I resumed my ride, and, after doubling a bluff headland, came suddenly on the beautiful bay of Djouni. The swelling slopes of Kesrouan flow gradually upward from the margin of the water to the peaks of Lebanon, crowned with the houses and villages of the Christians and Druses. Here and there a convent gleaming clear and white against the dark foliage and on the opposite horn of the bay, on the hillside rose the village of Djouni. It was partly hidden by trees and fir groves, the delicate blossoms of the cyclamen hung flowering from their variegated tufts in the crevices of the rocks, and the butterflies sported their little day in the glorious sunset, under which the waves had lulled to a murmuring ripple. It seems as if summer had burst from her icy prison to snatch another garland from the iron grasp of her tyrant. As I sauntered along, enjoying the loveliness of the view, I had forgotten my rest, and night overtook me by the time I had passed the south end of the bay. I was still eighteen miles from Beirut. The road was now too rugged to push on very fast. I reached Nahr el Kelb, flowing out of a steep gloomy mountain pass, the sides of which were so steep that the air struck cold, like going into an underground vault on entering it. I afterwards heard that the cliffs of Nahr el Kelb were full of Egyptian sculptures and inscriptions, and I regretted much having lost the opportunity of seeing them. Crossing over a bridge, I could just distinguish, by the expiring twilight, the appearance of an aqueduct or other excavations cut in the right-hand cliff. A shed on the other side of the bridge was occupied by people and cattle, which I was not sorry for, as it was too cold and damp to sleep in without taking a fever. I ascended the opposite cliff by steps cut in the rock and at last took refuge in a Greek shop after nine hours riding. A pillau made with samin (or what in England would be called rancid butter), and a duck, which I had shot on the road, roasted, made me quite a feast, and I was happy to be content with my quarters.

The morning of the 21st was fine, and it took me three hours via roads knee deep in mud, rendered worse by the constant passage of cattle, to reach Beirut, a large place with extensive uncovered bazaars and ill paved streets. As I wished to see something of the people, I put up in an upper room, in a large khan called the Kassaria. The lower part of the building was entirely occupied by silk merchants, who were sitting in their respective stores, reeling, twisting or spinning their silks, when not attending to customers, and surrounded by skeins and fabrics of all colours. They make a great variety of ornamental silk work, as braids, cords and tassels, purses, embroidered belts and horse trappings. In the centre of the courtyard grew an immense mulberry tree, an appropriate ornament for a silk bazaar.

Comments on the British Consular system...

I found here the same niggardliness and want of hospitality as I'd experienced on the part of our other English consul's in the Middle East. I regret this only for the sake of the English name; on my own account I'm not sorry for it, as it will obviate any scruples I might have felt in making a few remarks on our consular system, which might have been an invidious task had I experienced kindness from any of its members.

For a commercial and commonwealth nation like England, the consular establishment is its political frontier, and the individual situation of consuls is of the greatest importance as regards our relations with foreign powers. Through them intelligence is transmitted affecting the safety of our political and commercial interests, and through them, as the representatives of the nation, are negotiations transacted and differences settled. This would seem to imply the necessity of employing men of talent and experience in situations of such consequence, and yet the neglect of this branch of the service is notorious, to the great injury of our commercial and political interests.

Any man who has a claim either private or public, without respect to fitness or qualification, is considered good enough for consul; and this carelessness, added to the common practice of appointing native agents, who seldom do us much honour, has gone far towards causing the name of a British consul to be despised abroad. Again, with our men in office at home so much engrossed in party politics and struggles for power, that they can spare little time to attend to the details of our foreign relations or inclination to support their agents in maintaining the dignity of the nation abroad, or the privileges of their countrymen. The Consuls General are instructed to compromise insults, hush up complaints, and give the government as little trouble as possible, which orders they transmit to their subordinates; the consequence of which is, that the British name is no longer respected, and our flag, in many instances, insulted, as foreigners have discovered that it can be done with impunity.

What is the cause of the success of Russia in her aggressive diplomacy? She employs clever men as agents, who are to be met with in every quarter of the globe, and who are expected to forward, instead of to conceal, the intelligence they may obtain. What is the cause of the fast rising name of the United States? They watch over their growing influence, are jealous of the violation of their national rights, assert reparation for insult with firmness, and are respected.

The different agencies on the coasts of Turkey are in the hands of natives, who carry on a disgraceful traffic in British protection; they keep large establishments of translators and couriers, who pay high for their situations, paying themselves in return by fleecing travellers, monopolizing the hire of horses, and selling protection in a smaller way. The people buying protection call themselves consulate dependents, and cannot be taken for debts or punished for minor offences. As such, the people are afraid to offend them, dreading the consular vengeance, and thus the British name is made to screen crime. Many of our consuls are entirely controlled by unprincipled interpreters, who have obtained an ascendancy over them by making themselves indispensible. The fact of two brothers holding the situation of Chief Dragoman to the English and Russian embassies at Constantinople/Istanbul needs no comment, and has been often noticed. I must, however, give the native agents credit for more hospitality than the English consuls.

Some time ago the consular body at Alexandria took upon themselves to concoct and publish 12 articles for the regulation of consulates in Syria, which superseded the existing treaties and agreements. An Austrian Commissioner was sent over by this anomalous body to see its provisions carried into effect. To this official it was expected the British representatives would submit their authority and the concerns of their subjects. One of the stipulations required that any affairs with the government were to be transacted through the medium of Suleiman Pacha, a Frenchman in the Egyptian service, who, of course, has the interests of his own country most at heart, for which no one can blame him, but in the meantime ours would be sacrificed.

While on the subject, however, I cannot avoid noticing the spirited conduct of Mr Young, a newly appointed vice consul at Jerusalem, who has succeeded, although unsupported, in overcoming the many difficulties which were thrown in the way of his remaining there by the local authorities and the natives, and has at length established himself on a secure footing by asserting his rights with firmness, and supporting the honour of his country.

In France the consular establishment is, like any other service, on a grading system of merit. Every person who enters it being obliged to begin at the lowest grade of Chancellier or office secretary, from which their promotion continues in course of time, and they form part of the diplomatic body, rising according to their talents.

Since writing the above I found the following pertinent remarks in Col. Pasley's Military Policy: *"If anything can be lamented or reprobated in our own system of foreign affairs, it is that we have too frequently seen, acting in the capacity of British agents abroad, men either without knowledge of any kind; or who, if they have possessed any knowledge of commerce, have confined it merely to speculations for their own private advantage. Some of them, one would think, had not the proper use of their eyes: for when our generals have consulted them, previous to landing in a country where they had passed half their lives, they have been unable to give any account of it. That such things have happened will, I believe, be allowed by most officers of experience in the army. It is a point of duty with the authorised resident in a foreign country to make observations, for even without positive instructions to that effect, he ought to be prepared to answer all questions that may be put to him, and neglect of duty either from want of zeal or capacity is culpable."*

The 22nd being Sunday, I attended service at the American mission, where they educate a great number of the native children, 20 or 30 of whom were present. This is a great benefit to the merchants and other Europeans residing here, who, owing to their knowledge of English and accounts, employ these pupils as head servants and commercial clerks. These missionaries at first settled and carried on their work in Mt. Lebanon among the native Christians. However, having interfered too much with doctrinal points, they excited the jealousy of the native clergy, who accused them of proselytizing, and they were eventually obliged to move into the town.

It would be uncommon for a traveller in Syria to pass Djouni, without mentioning that extraordinary woman, who has been so long the heroine of its mountains, and I shall probably be the last as I can record her burial. Lady Hester Stanhope (1776 – 1839) may she rest in peace (she became chief of the household of her uncle, William Pitt the Younger, in his position as British Prime Minister and was a British socialite, adventurer and traveler. Her archaeological expedition to Ashkelon in 1815 is considered the first modern excavation in the history of Holy Land archeology). When intelligence was brought of her death, the consul went to her residence in the mountains, where he found the body laid out in a small darkened room, covered with a sheet and a single candle burning at the head and feet, partially lighting the forms and features of her Arab servants and dependents who surrounded the remains of their mistress. She was buried in her garden, at her own request by the American mission. Her effects were sold by auction. I saw the famous horses she had prized so much. One with a deformed hollow back was bought by an Arab for £2 or £3; the other, a white mare, was a beautiful creature, but had not been out of the stable for 17 years, was bought by the consul for £12.

Finding the accommodation in the Kassaria not altogether suitable we moved to an auberge kept by an Italian, and frequented by foreign merchant skippers, customhouse officers, and others of the same class, which was little better, and the cost as bad as need be.

Being the chief seaport in Syria, Beirut is crowded and populous. In addition to the usual variety of costume, the Druze woman have been often noticed, their veils being supported by horns of filigree silver, a foot and a half long. From all I can learn, I'm inclined to believe that the religion of the Druzes, which they endeavour to keep secret, is an idolatrous system synonymous with, or very nearly allied to, Brahminism. I have heard that the Druze pretend to be descended from the first Crusaders under Godfrey, but this is very improbable. I do not imagine that the scriptural expressions where horns are mentioned have any fanciful allusion to this costume, as some have tried to prove; but, as the Italians say,"Si non e vero e ben trovato". If it's not true, it's well founded.

I think it was in Paris that I saw a steam engine at work in a confiseur's shop, grinding chocolate. What would they say in Regent Street to a camel walking round turning a mill for grinding sugar for making sweetmeats? This I saw in a confectioners shop in Beirut.

It is astonishing to see the immense number of stone pillars of the ancient Berytus. The foundations of the quays at the waterside are composed of these pillars, laid in rows. The jetty or breakwater, enclosing the inner port for small craft, is also formed of these massive stone columns, laid horizontally on each other. The opposite side of the port is protected by a gloomy looking castle, which runs out into the sea, and is approached by a ruined passage on arches.

The cruelty of the governor Beirut, Mahmoud Bey, is a commentary on the vaunted improvement of the government under Mohammed Ali, and is equal in atrocity to the most unblushing acts of tyranny committed under the Turkish despotism, by the principles of which this country is still governed. Under some pretext, which is never wanting, but really for the purpose of extorting a large sum of money, a Christian saraff (money lender) was thrown into a dungeon and loaded with chains, with the addition of an iron spiked collar. A chain was passed through the grate of the cell, which the sentry or other person employed, had orders to jerk continually, until the wretched victim consented to pay the money. He was fastened in a position which prevented his moving, and this lingering torture was persevered with for several months, until it fortunately came to the knowledge of the European residents, who immediately combined to put a stop to this outrage on humanity. On their representation, the Pasha had the man released, and his case fairly investigated.

Giorgio, hearing of the length of our intended journey, lost heart, and refused to proceed any further. We accordingly discharged him and did not take on another in his place. He was a ready witted, intelligent fellow and at times insolent. In many respects superior to the rest of his class as he observed of himself with comparative truth - in allusion to the well-known character of his countrymen in the Levant," Ben che son Greco, son uomo onesto". Even if I'm Greek, I'm honest.

He spoke Turkish and Arabic, passing himself off among the unsophisticated villagers as a Muslim, he had been of great benefit to us thus far, but, as we had parted with our horses and lightened our luggage, a servant would now have been more an encumbrance than an advantage.

The Europeans here associate very little together, being an enmity with each other, and divided by petty jealousies, a common evil of small societies, and of more frequent occurrence in the Middle East, from the clashing of individual and national interests. In consequence of this we passed dull Christmas season, our consul keeping a closed house.

On 27 December we left Beirut, with two hired horses and a driver, following the rugged coast road at the foot of the Druze Mountains, the stronghold of the Emir Beshir, who is chief of all the mountain lands between here and Sidon. He lives at Dair el Kammar, and, although nominally independent, pays a tribute to Mohammed Ali on account of his having afforded him protection when the Sultan endeavoured to take his life. He governs approximately 1200 villages, and can bring a large force of horsemen into the field. He is said to have no avowed faith, but temporises, changing his profession to suit his political interests.

The mountains to the left presented a grand and imposing effect under a lowering sky. After a six hour ride, we stopped at a large khan, which we occupied in common with horses and mules. The night was a very cold, and one of the inmates bought a large pile of wood, which he proposed lighting in the centre of the floor. However, not wishing to be smoked out, we prevented this, and made ourselves warm in bed, and we were no sooner asleep than they substituted a heap of charcoal which they thought would not disturb us. The next morning I woke with a splitting headache and nausea, which I attributed to a bilious attack, little thinking of the actual cause. Although we used charcoal all the way to Jerusalem, during the whole of which time I was unwell, it was not till then that I discovered the real cause, and nearly paid dear for the experience.

The next morning it rained unmercifully, and we entered Sidon (Saida) after a three hour ride, and found accommodation at the house of a Greek. The town is situated on an elevated promontory, backed by the green hills of the Lebanon. The interior is gloomy and half in ruins: you find here nothing to remind you of its former grandeur, the few streets are narrow and intricate, and the population scanty. A few truncated stone columns are scattered about, and the ruins of a castle, said to have been built by Louis IX, of modern style, attest the sway of the Crusaders, and serve now to add picturesque charm to the view.

Hearing that Suleiman Pasha resided here, we called on him, and he insisted on our remaining and dining with him. His real name is Anselme Séves, but having professed to be a Moslem, he has raised himself by his talents and perseverance to the rank of Major General in the Egyptian army, which, in fact, he organised entirely himself. In the French service he entered the Navy at 12 years of age, and served five years, and then joined the Hussars in 1807: he served in the campaigns of 1809 in Austria, 1812 in Russia, 1813 in Germany, and 1814 in France. After 14 years service he was made a sous-lieutenant, and in 1814 was only a lieutenant of chasseurs, when, despairing of promotion, or for some other reason, he retired to Egypt and offered his services to Mohammed Ali.

He was employed mining and excavating ruins in the interior. However, having convinced the politic Pasha of the advantage and feasibility of establishing a regular army, and obtained his permission, he commenced his experiments in military, which succeeded so well that more hands were required and sent for, and the present disciplined army was raised under French, Italian, and Turkish officers. One of his cavalry regiments, which I had not an opportunity of seeing, is equipped in a cuirassier uniform, with a Phrygian helmet, the peak of which guards the nose.

Suleiman Pasha is now a hale veteran of fifty two, and a thorough Frenchman with Napoleon as his idol. One of his rooms is entirely hung with Napoleon portraits and prints of scenes from his life. At the upper end of the room is a large bust of the Emperor, crowned with a laurel wreath, and surrounded by trophies of the standards and arms taken from the Turks at the battle of Nezib, placed there, as he says, "pour faire homage à Napoleon". The rooms are papered with designs of groups of arms under which he has served in the French army, which form a very elegant pattern.

He was dressed in his Egyptian uniform, and his table was excellent, with abundance of wine and liqueurs. Besides ourselves, there was a French doctor and an old "comrade d'armes", who had come to pay him a visit, and he and the general talked over their campaigns and recapitulated their several exploits of former days, and we spent a very entertaining evening. Alluding to the eastern question, he said they were equally prepared for peace or war, that is, with the Turks, for he was not positive how his men might withstand European troops. He wished us to stay with him for a longer period, and was extremely kind and obliging; and as kindness of heart shows itself mostly in trifles, I cannot help mentioning that, knowing I was indisposed, he very considerately sent me a supply of eau de cologne before starting. He is currently occupied with building a new and extensive residence at Saida, supposing that affairs in the East are now settled. The environs of this place and Tsoor were lately infested by the Mutualis, a tribe of mountaineers who call themselves Soofis. They inhabit the southern districts of Lebanon, and are the dread of their neighbours, from their reputed deeds of cruelty and atrocity. They threatened to plunder these towns; but the Emir of the Druzes being applied to by the Pasha, succeeded in dispersing them, and the roads are now again open.

29 December 1839

It's a nine hour ride from Saida to Tsoor, and as we did not leave till midday, we had to perform a great part of this after midnight, which was rendered more unpleasant by rain. We had to cross marshes nearer the town and the road wound along the sandy beach. We passed the wreck of a vessel half buried in the sand, the ribs of which rose like spectres in the gloom, and a jackal skulked silently away from the water's edge, where he had been searching for fish or any prey the waves might throw up. At length, when nearly close to it, Tyre loomed black on our sight against the western sky. However, on reaching it, we were mortified to find the gates shut. It is surrounded by a wall as a protection against the plundering mountaineers.

After our pleading calls, the guards were induced to open the gates and let us in, and we wandered through the narrow dark bazaars. The guards could not leave their posts to show us the way, and with everyone else asleep, we were obliged to make a noisy commotion on the door of the most respectable house we could find. This bought the whole family to the upper window, who vented their astonishment in voices of every key, and being so unseasonably disturbed. At length we persuaded one to come down and conduct us to the house of the local British agent, where we were well received and treated with great hospitality. The next day the rain was incessant and overpowering, and it continued for three successive days, during which it was impossible to attempt to proceed. Just as well as I was very ill, and we considered ourselves fortunate in being in such good quarters.

The first night of our stop, as we were sitting round the fire, a commotion outside gave notice of the arrival of some more unlucky winter travellers, who joined our party, after changing their saturated garments. It proved to be the celebrated French painter, Horace Vernet, and two of his pupils. I'd seen his paintings in Paris when a boy and little expected to meet at such a time and place. He's a small, spare old man, full of spirits and activity, and very intelligent and entertaining. He wore the Egyptian uniform, with a large beard and moustache. He related a variety of anecdotes and stories with great humour, and we were not sorry at having the society of such an amusing companion during the time we stayed here, weather bound. He had with him a handsome gold sheathed sword, presented to him by the Emperor of Russia, with who he had been on intimate terms. It was rather a risk carrying this about with him, in case any of the Arab robbers had been tempted to relieve him of his extra baggage, but was characteristic, as well as his case of English duelling pistols, which could not be of much use while travelling. On hinting about this he observed, "Ma foi, on ne sait jamais ce qui peut arriver", We never know what can happen, alluding to the chance of a single combat. He was on his way to visit the localities of the battle of Nezib, between the Turks and Egyptians, which he intended to paint for the Pasha.

During the partial intervals of when the rain stopped, we ventured out to look on the spot where Tyre once stood. It certainly required the conviction arising from the truth of prophecy and the proof of history to believe and realise that there… across the restless waters, formerly rose the proud city, which, for 13 years, could withstand the power of Nebuchadnezzar, and, afterward, brave the genius of Alexander, at a time when he was refusing the sovereignty of Asia, west of Euphrates, offered him by the Persian monarch.

In calm, clear weather, it is said; the ruins may be seen and traced at the bottom of the sea from a boat, as well as the jetties which formed the two ports. ”She has died the death of them that are slain in the midst of the sea”. A few massive pillars among the rocks are the only remains of her former splendour. For 2000 years the waves have rolled over her, and the fishermen now cast their nets in her palaces, which lie deep in a watery grave. I sat on the seashore and contemplated the foam crested waves, leaping triumphantly above what once was Tyre. As I mused on the judgements and fate of the merchant city, a voice seemed to waft on the wings of the howling storm that swept over me, "Except ye repent, ye shall all likewise perish!" The present town of Tsoor, occupying a rocky promontory, is of little consequence: there are a few rather good houses, but, in general, they are mean and miserable. Outside the town is a remnant of an ancient aqueduct, which brought water from the hills and now lies nearly buried in the sand.

Edward's journey continues in the next book, "Palestine As It Was".

BY THE SAME AUTHOR

BRITISH POLICY IN THE MIDDLE EAST & THE CREATION OF ISRAEL
ISBN 1515087832 - £7.50 / €9.00

Talking of the Middle East, many think of Peter O'Toole and the famous Lawrence of Arabia. However, before him there was someone that also became the doyen of the British foreign office. Lawrence felt close to the Arabs and tried to create a pan-Arabic state, whereas Edward Mitford was driven towards creating a home for the Jewish nation.

Edward Mitford was the first British government official to present a plan to the ministers of the British government – well before Herzl, Balfour or Ben-Gurion and before the Zionist movement took form in Switzerland in 1897 – to share Palestine with one of the most creative and industrious people in Europe. His plan ultimately led to the Balfour Declaration. It lays out the practicalities and process of achieving an independent state with regards to worldwide opinion, the position of Russia and other European countries and their influence in the Middle East. Edward died five years before the Balfour Declaration of 2 November 1917.

Everything detailed in Edward's appeal and the plan he presented in 1845 took place and happened – it set the framework for the British mandate that followed in 1920 to 1948. His life and work is part of English history and cannot continue to be hidden from public knowledge. Originally published by J Hatchard & Son, 187 Piccadilly, London, in 1845, it has remained out of print due to family indifference.

Today, Edward Mitford's great-great grandson, Hugh Mitford Raymond, author of The Mitford Family, see over page, presents the untold story of the creation of Israel. The reason he has republished the work of his great-great grandfather is purely historical and far from any debate. Obviously times have changed, the situation in the Middle East is not the same but the text reveals the mentalities of the time, the philosophies and the "festering germs" of later decisions.

This book is a historic testimony of a project which anchors in time much of the current events even today. This book allows the reader to better understand the reasons of British presence in the Middle East, its politics and policy, its diplomacy, its implication and the responsibilities in the conflicts to come over a land promised to two peoples - so different yet so similar.

Finally, the reader will not miss the amazing contrast between Edward Mitford and his quest to create a homeland for the Jewish nation – to the pro Nazi and fascist commitments of Diana and Unity Mitford, two of the famous and infamous Mitford sisters. Diana divorced Bryan Guinness of the Guinness Brewery fortune to marry Sir Oswald Mosley, leader of the British Union of Fascists and Unity became intimately involved with Hitler and his anti-Semitic ideas until her failed attempt at committing suicide, when Hitler sent her back to England via Switzerland.

MITFORD LITERARY SOCIETY

THE MITFORD FAMILY
ISBN 9781903506448 - £16.99 / €20.00

It's not just about those aristocratic and scandalous Mitford girls! From the beginning of England to the disintegration of the family seat in the 21st century - landowners and philanthropists, writers and historians, activists and fascists and peers of the realm feature in one of the world's most fascinating dynasties. The Mitford family of Mitford, Northumberland and the succession of lords and squires that have overseen Mitford Castle, Mitford Manor, Mitford Hall, Mitford Church and surrounding farmlands since before the Norman conquest in 1066.

From the words, carved into the stone wall of Mitford Castle dungeon, "Captivus Morior 141" (Captive I Die)….. to the gallant support of Roger Bertram to force King John to sign the Magna Carta at Runnymede in 1215, only to have Mitford village and church burnt with all the villagers inside – the Mitford dynasty continued its never ending saga and adventure from the beginning of England and British Empire to a dismal ending of perfect indifference in the 21st century.

From establishing the first hospital on the subcontinent of India (Mitford Hospital, Dhaka, Bangladesh) to the very heart and soul of British culture and politics in London. John Mitford edited and published the works of English poets, Milton, Swift, Parnell, Young, Lamb, Wordsworth, Byron and Gray. Edward Mitford FRGS, British government official and specialist on the Middle East was the first person to ride 7000 miles on horseback through 16 countries from London to Ceylon (now Sri Lanka) and present the plan for the creation of Israel to the ministers of the British government.

From Edward's quest to create a homeland for the Jewish nation to the pro Nazi and fascist commitments of Diana and Unity Mitford, two of the famous and infamous Mitford sisters. Diana divorced Bryan Guinness of the Guinness Brewery fortune to marry Sir Oswald Mosley, leader of the British Union of Fascists and Unity became intimate friends with Hitler. Deborah Mitford became Duchess of Devonshire. Bertram Mitford FRGS, a founder of South African literature, was the first person to travel around South Africa to interview the survivors of the Zulu War at Isandlwana, the worst defeat of the British during the Victorian era. Bertram wrote 44 bestselling novels, covering the history and culture of South Africa. From Europe to the Middle East and Africa, to Japan and China, Australia and New Zealand, you'll find the name Mitford.

Today, from family archives, South African born Hugh Mitford Raymond, great-great grandson, nephew and cousin to the last seven squires of Mitford since 1042, presents the untold story of the Mitford family of Mitford, Northumberland. The estate originally covered over 50,000 acres and has been owned and lived on by 32 generations of the Mitford family for 964 years until it was sold in 1993 due to no heir being found. The dynasty ended with the death of the last squire in 2002.

This book reveals the untold, hidden face of the Mitford family. If you enjoy true life history, read the facts and events leading up the tragic ending of nearly 1000 years of family heritage along with the intrigue, betrayal and all that goes with the real thing - you be the judge? To quote the words inscribed on his great-great grandfather's gravestone in Mitford churchyard "There the tears of earth are dried – there the hidden things are clear".

Books available from all good bookshops and Amazon.

Born and brought up in South Africa, Hugh grew up on the back of a horse and went on to train and breed racehorses. He has served in the South African Defence Force completing active duties in Mozambique, Caprivi Strip and South West Africa. He also managed large farming operations in Zimbabwe. Widely travelled he has lived in 6 countries and speaks 4 languages, working for various international companies, along with IBM and United Nations. He has been resident in the South of France for over 20 years and has served on the central committee of the British Association (Menton, Nice, Cannes & Var) linked with the British Consulate for 15 years, providing help to British residents along the Riviera. He is a member of the London Society of Authors and Chairman of the South African International Association of the Riviera. Hugh is the great-great grandson, nephew and cousin to the last seven squires of Mitford, on the direct mainline of the Mitford family of Mitford since 1042.